"I saw your glory
and it dazzled me."
- St. Augustine

Date _____   **Speaker** _____

Topic _____

Scripture References
_____
_____

My Notes:

What "Speaks" To Me:

What I Will Implement This Week:

For Further Study:

Date

Speaker

Topic

Scripture References

My Notes:

What "Speaks" To Me:

What I Will Implement This Week:

For Further Study:

Date

Speaker

Topic

Scripture References

My Notes:

What "Speaks" To Me:

For Further Study:

What I Will Implement This Week:

Date _____   **Speaker** _____

Topic _____

Scripture References

My Notes:

What "Speaks" To Me:

What I Will Implement This Week:

For Further Study:

Date _____ **Speaker** _____

Topic _____

Scripture References
_____
_____

My Notes:

What "Speaks" To Me:

For Further Study:

What I Will Implement This Week:

Date _____   **Speaker** _____

Topic _____

Scripture References
_____
_____

My Notes:

What "Speaks" To Me:

What I Will Implement This Week:

For Further Study:

Date _____   **Speaker** _____

Topic _____

Scripture References

_____

_____

My Notes:

What "Speaks" To Me:

What I Will Implement This Week:

For Further Study:

Date _____   **Speaker** _____

Topic _____

Scripture References

_____
_____

My Notes:	What "Speaks" To Me:

For Further Study:

What I Will Implement This Week:

Date _____   **Speaker** _____

Topic _____

Scripture References

My Notes:

What "Speaks" To Me:

What I Will Implement This Week:

For Further Study:

Date _____   **Speaker** _____

Topic _____

Scripture References
_____
_____

My Notes:

What "Speaks" To Me:

What I Will Implement This Week:

For Further Study:

Date _____ **Speaker** _____

Topic _____

Scripture References
_____
_____

My Notes:
_____
_____
_____
_____
_____
_____
_____
_____
_____
_____
_____
_____
_____
_____

What "Speaks" To Me:
_____
_____
_____
_____
_____
_____
_____
_____
_____

For Further Study:
_____
_____
_____

What I Will Implement This Week:
_____
_____
_____
_____
_____
_____
_____

Date

Speaker

Topic

Scripture References

My Notes:

What "Speaks" To Me:

What I Will Implement This Week:

For Further Study:

Date _____   **Speaker** _____

Topic _____

Scripture References
_____
_____

My Notes:

What "Speaks" To Me:

What I Will Implement This Week:

For Further Study:

Date _____ **Speaker** _____

Topic _____

Scripture References

_____

_____

My Notes:

What "Speaks" To Me:

What I Will Implement This Week:

For Further Study:

Date _____ **Speaker** _____

Topic _____

Scripture References
_____
_____

My Notes:

What "Speaks" To Me:

What I Will Implement This Week:

For Further Study:

Date _____   **Speaker** _____

Topic _____

Scripture References

_____

_____

My Notes:

What "Speaks" To Me:

What I Will Implement This Week:

For Further Study:

Date _____   **Speaker** _____

Topic _____

Scripture References
_____
_____

My Notes:

What "Speaks" To Me:

What I Will Implement This Week:

For Further Study:

Date _____   **Speaker** _____

Topic _____

Scripture References

My Notes:

What "Speaks" To Me:

What I Will Implement This Week:

For Further Study:

Date _____   **Speaker** _____

Topic _____

Scripture References
_____
_____

My Notes:

What "Speaks" To Me:

What I Will Implement This Week:

For Further Study:

Date

Speaker

Topic

Scripture References

My Notes:

What "Speaks" To Me:

What I Will Implement This Week:

For Further Study:

Date _____ **Speaker** _____

Topic _____

Scripture References

_____
_____

My Notes:

What "Speaks" To Me:

For Further Study:

What I Will Implement This Week:

Date _____   **Speaker** _____

Topic _____

Scripture References
_____
_____

My Notes:
_____
_____
_____
_____
_____
_____
_____
_____
_____
_____
_____
_____
_____

For Further Study:
_____
_____
_____
_____

What "Speaks" To Me:
_____
_____
_____
_____
_____
_____
_____
_____
_____
_____

What I Will Implement This Week:
_____
_____
_____
_____
_____
_____
_____

Date

Speaker

Topic

Scripture References

My Notes:

What "Speaks" To Me:

What I Will Implement This Week:

For Further Study:

Date _____   **Speaker** _____

Topic _____

Scripture References
_____
_____

My Notes:

What "Speaks" To Me:

What I Will Implement This Week:

For Further Study:

Date _____ **Speaker** _____

Topic _____

Scripture References
_____
_____

My Notes:

What "Speaks" To Me:

What I Will Implement This Week:

For Further Study:

Date _____   **Speaker** _____

Topic _____

Scripture References
_____
_____

My Notes:

What "Speaks" To Me:

What I Will Implement This Week:

For Further Study:

Date

Speaker

Topic

Scripture References

My Notes:

What "Speaks" To Me:

What I Will Implement This Week:

For Further Study:

Date

Speaker

Topic

Scripture References

My Notes:

What "Speaks" To Me:

What I Will Implement This Week:

For Further Study:

Date _____   **Speaker** _____

Topic _____

Scripture References

_____
_____

My Notes:	What "Speaks" To Me:

For Further Study:

What I Will Implement This Week:

Date _____   **Speaker** _____

Topic _____

Scripture References

My Notes:

What "Speaks" To Me:

What I Will Implement This Week:

For Further Study:

Date _____   **Speaker** _____

Topic _____

Scripture References

_____

My Notes:	What "Speaks" To Me:

For Further Study:	What I Will Implement This Week:

Date _____ **Speaker** _____

Topic _____

Scripture References

My Notes:

What "Speaks" To Me:

What I Will Implement This Week:

For Further Study:

Date _____   **Speaker** _____

Topic _____

Scripture References
_____
_____

My Notes:

What "Speaks" To Me:

What I Will Implement This Week:

For Further Study:

Date _____   **Speaker** _____

Topic _____

Scripture References

_____

_____

My Notes:

What "Speaks" To Me:

What I Will Implement This Week:

For Further Study:

Date _____ **Speaker** _____

Topic _____

Scripture References
_____
_____

My Notes:

For Further Study:

What "Speaks" To Me:

What I Will Implement This Week:

Date _____ **Speaker** _____

Topic _____

Scripture References

_____

My Notes:

What "Speaks" To Me:

What I Will Implement This Week:

For Further Study:

Date

Speaker

Topic

Scripture References

My Notes:

What "Speaks" To Me:

What I Will Implement This Week:

For Further Study:

Date

Speaker

Topic

Scripture References

My Notes:

What "Speaks" To Me:

What I Will Implement This Week:

For Further Study:

Date _____ **Speaker** _____

Topic _____

Scripture References
_____
_____

My Notes:

What "Speaks" To Me:

What I Will Implement This Week:

For Further Study:

Date _____   **Speaker** _____

Topic _____

Scripture References

My Notes:

What "Speaks" To Me:

What I Will Implement This Week:

For Further Study:

Date _____   **Speaker** _____

Topic _____

Scripture References
_____
_____

My Notes:

What "Speaks" To Me:

What I Will Implement This Week:

For Further Study:

Date _____   **Speaker** _____

Topic _____

Scripture References

_____

_____

My Notes:

What "Speaks" To Me:

What I Will Implement This Week:

For Further Study:

Date _____   **Speaker** _____

Topic _____

Scripture References
_____
_____

My Notes:

What "Speaks" To Me:

What I Will Implement This Week:

For Further Study:

Date _____   **Speaker** _____

Topic _____

Scripture References
_____
_____

My Notes:

For Further Study:

What "Speaks" To Me:

What I Will Implement This Week:

Date _____   **Speaker** _____

Topic _____

Scripture References

_____
_____

My Notes:

What "Speaks" To Me:

What I Will Implement This Week:

For Further Study:

Date _____   **Speaker** _____

Topic _____

Scripture References

My Notes:

What "Speaks" To Me:

What I Will Implement This Week:

For Further Study:

Date _____   **Speaker** _____

Topic _____

Scripture References

_____
_____

My Notes:

What "Speaks" To Me:

What I Will Implement This Week:

For Further Study:

Date _____ **Speaker** _____

Topic _____

Scripture References
_____
_____

My Notes:	What "Speaks" To Me:

For Further Study:

What I Will Implement This Week:

Date _____   **Speaker** _____

Topic _____

Scripture References
....
....

My Notes:	What "Speaks" To Me:

For Further Study:	What I Will Implement This Week:

Date _____   **Speaker** _____

Topic _____

Scripture References
_____
_____

My Notes:

What "Speaks" To Me:

What I Will Implement This Week:

For Further Study:

Date _____   **Speaker** _____

Topic _____

Scripture References
_____
_____

My Notes:

For Further Study:

What "Speaks" To Me:

What I Will Implement This Week:

Date _____   **Speaker** _____

Topic _____

Scripture References

_____
_____

My Notes:	What "Speaks" To Me:

For Further Study:	What I Will Implement This Week:

Made in the USA
Middletown, DE
17 December 2021